# READING THE WATER

Other volumes in the series:

*The Morse Poetry Prize*
*Edited by Guy Rotella*

CHARLES HARPER WEBB

# Reading
# the Water

THE 1997 MORSE
POETRY PRIZE
🌿 SELECTED AND
INTRODUCED BY
EDWARD HIRSCH

*Northeastern University Press*
BOSTON

Northeastern University Press

*Library of Congress Cataloging-in-Publication Data*

Webb, Charles Harper.
      Reading the water / Charles Harper Webb ; selected and introduced
by Edward Hirsch.
          p.   cm. — (Morse Poetry Prize ; 1997)
      ISBN 1-55553-325-6 (pbk.)
      I. Hirsch, Edward.   II. Title.   III. Series.
PS3573.E194R4     1997
811'.54—dc21                        97-28802

Designed by Ann Twombly

Composed in Weiss by Graphic Composition, Athens, Georgia. Printed and bound by Thomson-Shore, Inc., Dexter, Michigan. The paper is Glatfelter Supple Opaque Recycled, an acid-free sheet.

MANUFACTURED IN THE UNITED STATES OF AMERICA
01   00   99   98   97      5   4   3   2   1

*In memory of my parents*
*and*
*for Karen*

ACKNOWLEDGMENTS

I would like to thank the editors of the following publications for first publishing these poems, sometimes in another version:

| | |
|---|---|
| *Agni* | "In the War Zone," "Behaviorists" |
| *Amelia* | "Without Being a Wimp" |
| *American Poetry Review* | "The Mummy Meets Hot-Headed Naked Ice-Borers" |
| *Ann Arbor Review* | "Girl at a Window" |
| *Exquisite Corpse* | "Perspective" |
| *5 A.M.* | "The Reasonable Man" |
| *Florida Review* | "The Death of Santa Claus" |
| *The Gettysburg Review* | "Broken Toe," "Evil Genius," "Temptations of Pinocchio" |
| *Green Mountains Review* | "How Lizzie Died" |
| *Gridlock* | "Spirits" |
| *Harvard Review* | "Umbrellas" |
| *The Iowa Review* | "My Muse" |
| *Laurel Review* | "The Dead Run" |
| *Louisville Review* | "Heat Death" |
| *Madison Review* | "Nature Poem" |
| *Michigan Quarterly Review* | "The Shape of History," "Twenty Years Late to See *The Rocky Horror Picture Show*," "Fantasy Girl" |
| *Paris Review* | "Marilyn's Machine," "In Praise of Pliny" |
| *Passages North* | "Poem for the Future," "Health" |
| *Ploughshares* | "True Prophets" |
| *Poet Lore* | "According to the Rule," "Reading the Water" |
| *Poetry East* | "Spiders," "What the Poets Would Have Done for You" |
| *Poetry Miscellany* | "Once Bitten" |
| *Puerto del Sol* | "Four-Wheeling" |

| | |
|---|---|
| *Quarterly West* | "The Crane Boy," "Buyer's Remorse," "Eating" |
| *Southern Poetry Review* | "Peaches," "You Missed the Earthquake, Bill" |
| *Tsunami* | "Prayer for the Man Who Mugged My Father, 72" |
| *Virginia Quarterly Review* | "One Story" |
| *West Branch* | "Blind" |
| *Western Humanities Review* | "Mastery," "Holiday Inn" |
| *Witness* | "Optimism" |

"Back Flip" reprinted by permission of the *Antioch Review*, vol. 51, no. 2 (Winter 1993). Copyright © 1993 by Charles H. Webb.

"Invocation to Allen as the Muse Euterpe" reprinted by permission of the *Antioch Review*, vol. 54, no. 3 (Summer 1996). Copyright © 1996 by Charles H. Webb.

"Flying Fish in the Jet Stream" appeared in the Chester H. Jones Foundation's *National Poetry Competition Winners, 1995.*

The writing of this book was partially funded by California State University, Long Beach, Scholarly and Creative Activities Awards.

Special thanks to Walter Pavlich, Phillip Levine, Robert Pinsky, Alberto Rios, Diane Wakoski, David St. John, Lynn Emanuel, Ron Koertge, Pattiann Rogers, Suzanne Lummis, Kurt Brown, Laure-Anne Bosselaar, Dinah Berland, and Richard Garcia.

# Contents

## PART III

# Introduction

Charles Harper Webb has a wild inventive energy, a quirky, at times even manic wit, and a deep sense of wonder at the world. His poems are filled with curiosities, with odd facts and details, with unlikely anecdotes—all of which he takes personally. As a poet, he's a wise-acre, a troublemaker—part stand-up comic, part anthropologist, part visionary. He is funny and takes gleeful pleasure in sending up various cultural illusions, stereotypes, and fantasies—especially his own. He can be withering about contemporary life; his irony gives him no rest. And yet he is a romantic despite himself: a singer of tales, a poet of praise.

The poems in *Reading the Water* are lucid, quick-talking, and shapely. The author has a certain brash linguistic charm, like someone who has talked his way into a formal gathering without an invitation. He knows how to get around once he's inside the door, but he carries with him a lot of suppressed rage. He's tempted to bring down certain childhood icons ("The Death of Santa Claus," "The Temptations of Pinocchio") and gets a bright frisson in intermingling high and low culture, high and low dictions. Among other things, he's an L.A. shrink, a purveyor of the schlock of postmodern culture, an ethnographer of the general populace's drift toward "video games, MTV, / and shopping malls" ("True Prophets"). It's characteristic of him to invoke his muse as the antiheroic author of an unpublished book called *Everyday Outrages* ("My Muse"). And yet he also loves the natural world, and finds nothing less than his own soul renewed in learning its language, in "reading the water."

One of Webb's favorite tactics is to confront the transcendental with the mundane, and vice versa—he goes in both directions. In his poem "Health," for example, the impulse to rapture is inevitably punctured:

"Be ecstatic," you tell yourself every so often;
but you're peeved at potholes in the street;
and one day your left arm is numb.

But so, too, the banal can be radiated by the transcendental. Typi-
cally, a broken toe sends him into a paroxysm of obscenities, "a word
orgasm after long celibacy." How oddly wonderful, he tells us (in
"Broken Toe"), that a seemingly small thing like a broken toe can
fracture the daily monotony. Thus he calls out:

Welcome back, pain. Welcome back, passion.
Welcome back, something-to-howl-about,

grist for the *how're-you-doing?* mill. Remind me
of the joys of walking, jump-rope, running,
playing footsie. Hammer home the certainty
of decay, memento mori at my body's end.

For all his defensive irony and wit, Webb ends up scoffing at
the scoffers. Watching Allen Ginsberg prancing around the stage—
embarrassing, vulnerable, completely present—he is reminded of the
large, open-hearted poet he had always meant to become ("Invoca-
tion to Allen as the Muse Euterpe"). He admits to his own petty
grievances and spiritual limitations, and calls for a kind of heart trans-
plant. Outlining Pliny's book of wonders, *Historia Naturalis*, he knows
too well that Pliny never could have conceived "of people lacking all
belief, devoid of wonder—// two-dimensional people who scoff at
everything" ("In Praise of Pliny"). He refuses to let himself become
like those people. And driving down Highway 5 he comes across the
place where the artist Christo is taking down hundreds of umbrellas
mushrooming across the landscape. The artist is depressed, he says,
because one had speared a spectator. At the conclusion of the poem
("Umbrellas") the speaker turns to his lover and declares:

Stand with me, my beauty, in the wind.
Let us think of Art and blood tests

before marriage, and how love may come,
at any instant, flying through the air
to pierce our neck or skull or lungs or heart.

The poems in *Reading the Water* move easily, fluidly, between the city and the country, helping to restore our sense of wonder at both realms. I'm moved by the way that this book, through whatever roundabout and even tortuous routes, keeps coming back refreshed to our strange, tenuous, and imperiled planet.

EDWARD HIRSCH

PART I

# The Mummy Meets Hot-Headed Naked Ice-Borers

Djedmaatesankh—temple musician, wife of Paankhntof,
daughter of Shedtaope—died childless, aged thirty-five,
in the tenth century B.C., of blood poisoning
from an abscessed incisor. CAT scans
of her mummy show how the abscess chewed
a walnut-sized hole in her upper jaw, gnawing

bone the way the creatures called "hot-headed
naked ice-borers" gnaw tunnels through
Antarctic ice. Six inches long, hairless and pink,
they look in pictures like sea lions with tumors
on their foreheads, and saber-teeth. The teeth
chew tunnels; the "tumors" are lumps of bone,

the skin of which writhes with blood vessels
radiating heat. Their normal temperature
is 110 degrees. Djedmaatesankh's fever
may have reached 104. One shot of penicillin
could have saved her, but it was 3000 years away.
Knowing about ice-borers might have saved French

explorer Philippe Poisson, who disappeared in 1837.
At five-foot-six, he could have been a large penguin:
the ice-borers' favorite food. A pack collects
under a penguin and, with their foreheads,
melts the ice it's standing on. The penguin sinks
as in quicksand; the borers attack like piranha,

leaving behind only beak, feathers, and feet—
as if the bird has taken them off before bed. Think
of Poisson, torn into fragments by their fangs.
Think of Djedmaatesankh in the three weeks the abscess
took to kill her. How did her husband feel,
hearing her scream? Watching her corpse carried

to the embalmers? Seeing the molded likeness
of her face rise from her pupal coffin? Did he weep
to lose his only love? Was he relieved
that he could remarry, and possibly have sons?
Or had mistresses provided those?
Did his wife's death make him curse, thank, cease

believing in his gods? Did Poisson's wife in Paris
dream of penguin beaks, feathers, feet encased
in ice? Did she see pink squirming things
with Phillipe's face? The first night Djedmaatesankh
went to bed with a toothache, did she dream
she was in a room crowded with people in strange clothes,

and while a white-skinned boy looked down at her
through a transparent wall like frozen air, making noises
that sounded like "Eeoo, gross," his sister began to scream,
and had to be carried outside, and that night
dreamed of Djedmaatesankh walking toward her,
gauze dripping from her shrivelled, childless hands?

# Health

You wake each morning in a satin bed—
the air caressing, temperature, humidity
just right—but the mail comes. You suck
down ripe papayas on your balcony
as lemon finches, scarlet tanagers,
black mynahs flicker through hibiscus
and the sea shrugs its white shoulders
in the sun—but wind keeps messing up
your hair. You swim through ocean
warm as skin, drifting with fish vivid
as the sunsets here, violet, orange,
claret, indigo, watching golden cowries
flow on black mantles across white coral—
but you scrape your hand on lava outside
the room where your love waits, limpid with sleep.

"Be ecstatic," you tell yourself every so often;
but you're peeved at potholes in the street;
and one day your left arm is numb. You lose
your balance for no reason, or feel faint,
or wake from bad dreams with a headache
that won't quit, or take your yearly physical,
leave feeling fine, then get a call
from a nurse who won't say why, but insists
you see the doctor right away. And right
away you're on a plane, one among rows
of faces watching desperately the last
green mountains disappear, and clouds close
over turquoise seas the way a woman
you still love, whom you betrayed, shuts
her robe in front of you for the last time.

## Perspective

A planeload of insurance salesmen, blown off course,
Discovers a tribe who believe an elephant-
In-the-distance is the same size as a gnat-in-the-eye.

This should cause trouble in a hunt. But tribespeople
Merely flick the pesky trumpeter away,
While the gnat—felled by clouds of arrows—feeds

The tribe for weeks. Faced by a lion, tribesmen run
until its head is small enough to squish. Muscular
Warriors are found dead, pierced by mosquito-needles

Ear-to-ear. Everything here is as it seems.
The stick-in-water, drawn out, remains crooked
As a boomerang. Mountain and molehill are identical.

Tragedies that crush Americans—love's waterbed
Popping; parents dropped into the scalding pot of age—
Require only that the sufferer walk away. "It's not so awful,"

Tribal healers say. "With every step, troubles shrink;
Their howling dwindles to a buzz; their fangs shrivel to the size
Of pollen grains. Reach out. Brush them away. You see?"

# Subatomic Particles

They have mellifluous names—*muon, gluon, baryon,*
the horny, anagrammatic *hadron*—because physicists
are poets with black glasses, calculator watches,
Bozo hair. Bullied at school, they speak in secret
tongues today, describing weapons of mass devastation.

"Three quarks for Muster Mark," James Joyce said
in *Finnegans Wake* (itself a weapon), and *quarks*
joined *leptons* and *photons* as "fundamental."
*Up, down, top, bottom, strange,* and *charm quarks,*
to be precise. Though, that small, nothing is precise.

Part-wave, part-particle, these cosmic iotae are only
metaphors in mathematics' poetry: *WIMPs* (weakly
interacting massive particles); *bosons, mesons, neutrinos*
blipping in and out of being, changing into energy
and back like girls unsure what to wear on a first date,

which could as easily be the last; time's kind of iffy
in the subatomic world. Location, too. It's lucky
"girls-on-a-date" is a metaphor; they couldn't tell
their parents where they'd be, except in probabilities.
"There's a 70% chance I'll be home by midnight."

Mom would have grounded me for that, even
with a note from Heisenberg, Father of Uncertainty.
The matter/antimatter issue invites a male/female analogy.
But while male and female join to make new life,
matter and antimatter mutually annihilate.

Think Jews & Arabs, Irish Catholics & Protestants.
Think *world's worst blind date.* Remember,
metaphors are not "reality." (What's that?)
My love is not, in most ways, like a red, red rose.
Still, the words make her blush and bloom.

Still, when NASA sends a satellite to Neptune,
it arrives. Still, the tiny whatsits leave their trails,
and gather into atoms, which—slowed enough—
become the fuzzy, loveable "Bose-Einstein condensate"—
everywhere and no one place at the same time,

like God. This was predicted mathematically,
though not everyone agreed. There's as much squabbling
among scientists as among poets, theologians,
congressmen. Reputations are at stake. And prizes.
And the fate of nations, if engineers find a theory to sink

incisors into. We can't stop them; still we must be science-
literate so that, if someone says "astrology,"
we know what's coming—if someone says "lepton,"
we won't mention four-leaf clovers or pots of gold.
So that, knowing quarks have (metaphoric) "color"—

red, blue, green—we can see even a dog pile
or lump of navel lint as rubies, sapphires, emeralds
blazing. So that we can picture love, which is a kind
of energy, flashing toward us through the air
like glittering arrows from mini-nano-bows.

So that, intellectually at least, we know
that our computers, TVs, microwaves, CAT scans,
and bombs don't run on Black Magic, but on the same
substance/not substance that makes/unmakes us
in this radiant world with and without end.

# Flying Fish in the Jet Stream

*One minute he was beside me; the next, he was gone.*
—Army buddy of Charles Casey Webb, 1880–1916

I pictured him bombed into a red mist
rising above the battlefield, filling the air.
Others kids' grandfathers took us fishing,
or to state parks in their mobile homes,
but mine was like God: everywhere.

His sword and sergeant's helmet
shone like sunlight high in the loblolly pines.
I heard his voice when redwing blackbirds
screamed and flashed their epaulets.
He had an English accent—said "I say!"

and "Cheerio," and called things "bloody,"
which colored them bright red. Summer nights,
I'd lie in the warm current of the attic fan,
and feel his fingers in the sweaty wind.
When anything was made in Germany—

a clock or Christmas ornament or Pfeffernusse—
I felt him there. His one thin comma
of black hair seemed glued onto his shiny head.
Pushing, bald-pated, between heaven
and earth hurt his brain, he said.

"Be a strong groundhog," he whispered
in dreams. "Flying fish in the jet stream."
(I interpreted that for days.) When Mom
sent me to my room, he taught me looks
to make her feel sorry and give me ice cream.

Crouched on the john, my twelfth birthday,
I saw a lone hair sprouting
like a black scratch above my little wang.
"Bye, Charlie boy," the pines,
the breeze, a redwing blackbird sang.

## The Death of Santa Claus

He's had chest pains for weeks,
but doctors don't make house
calls to the North Pole,

he's let his Blue Cross lapse,
blood tests make him faint,
hospital gowns always flap

open, waiting rooms upset
his stomach, and it's only
indigestion anyway, he thinks,

until, feeding the reindeer,
he feels as if a monster fist
has grabbed his heart and won't

stop squeezing. He can't
breathe, and the beautiful white
world he loves goes black,

and he drops on his jelly belly
in the snow and Mrs. Claus
tears out of the toy factory

wailing, and the elves wring
their little hands, and Rudolph's
nose blinks like a sad ambulance

light, and in a tract house
in Houston, Texas, I'm 8,
telling my mom that stupid

kids at school say Santa's a big
fake, and she sits with me
on our purple-flowered couch,

and takes my hand, tears
in her throat, the terrible
news rising in her eyes.

# Prayer for the Man
## Who Mugged My Father, 72

May there be an afterlife.

May you meet him there, the same age as you.
May the meeting take place in a small, locked room.

May the bushes where you hid be there again, leaves tipped with
    razorblades and acid.
May the rifle butt you bashed him with be in his hands.
May the glass in his car window, which you smashed as he sat
    stopped at a red light, be embedded in the rifle butt and on the
    floor to break your fall.

May the needles the doctors used to close his eye, stab your pupils
    every time you hit the wall and then the floor, which will be
    often.
May my father let you cower for a while, whimpering, "Please don't
    shoot me. Please."
May he laugh, unload your gun, toss it away;
Then may he take you with bare hands.

May those hands, which taught his son to throw a curve and drive
    a nail and hold a frog, feel like cannonballs against your jaw.
May his arms, which powered handstands and made their muscles
    jump to please me, wrap your head and grind your face like
    stone.
May his chest, thick and hairy as a bear's, feel like a bear's snapping
    your bones.
May his feet, which showed me the flutter kick and carried me
    miles through the woods, feel like axes crushing your one claim
    to manhood as he chops you down.

And when you are down, and he's done with you, which will be
    soon, since, even one-eyed, with brain damage, he's a merciful
    man,

11

May the door to the room open and let him stride away to the
    Valhalla he deserves.
May you—bleeding, broken—drag yourself upright.

May you think the worst is over;
You've survived, and may still win.

Then may the door open once more, and let me in.

# You Missed the Earthquake, Bill

One instant I was asleep in bed; the next,
I was bucking and bouncing like a tuna
on the floor. Power-transformers flashed
like bombs; then black poured in. "Oh shit, oh shit,"
I prayed until the jolting stopped. Alive,

my house standing—as far as I could tell—
I groped for clothes, and stumbled into them
outside, where car-alarms whooped
and caterwauled in pre-dawn chill. The yellow
feelers of flashlights twitched up and down

the black trees, black sidewalk, black street.
Art Campo's radio reported freeways buckled,
buildings down, exploded gas lines,
spewing water mains. We tried to think
we were lucky as aftershocks rolled in

like bowling balls. When I think of you, Bill,
I usually think of some good thing you're missing:
redheads, pow-wows, barbecues, thunderstorms,
the Hubble telescope tuning in a cosmos clear
enough to see the souls in heaven. (I didn't

see you.) But the dead miss bad things too—
getting fired from a good job, which I just was,
or dumped by a woman you love,
which I was too, or trapped in your apartment's
rubble or your mini-van, screaming

as chunks of overpass crush it, then you.
I thought I heard your kids crying three blocks
away as darkness grabbed our homes and shook,
your wife—still hating you for Jane in Idaho—
screaming, "Goddamn it, Bill, why aren't you here?!"

A cop was motorcycling through silvery fog
when a freeway bridge dropped out
from under him. Dying, he missed a week
of sixteen-hour shifts, rescues, crushed bodies,
looters, gapers, gorgers on misfortune.

He might've liked those things, who knows?
We never know what we've enjoyed till we look back.
He was too startled, probably, to enjoy
his arcing flight, then too afraid. But what
a ride he must have had, Bill, what a ride.

# Spiders

They drift through darkness, eight-fingered
hands grasping for your eyes.

In daylight they occur like accidents,
suddenly *there*. They are fear's footprint

on the shower floor, its rune stamped
on the wall. Small, hopping nightmares,

scuttling aliens, they charge at you
with scrabbly legs, jaws dripping pain.

Masters of treachery, they leap from hiding,
paralyze their prey, then suck it dry.

Creeping out from dusty corners, cracks in walls,
they are your landlords when the lights die.

Fuzzy succubae, they sleep with you;
leave itchy kisses where they've been.

Walking to the bathroom, 2 a.m., your feet tickle.
Don't hit the light switch. Don't look down.

It's not enough to spray them with Black Flag;
they must be drowned in it.

It's not enough to crush one gently.
Grind it underfoot until it disappears.

Yet they are beautiful: furry as buffalo,
long-limbed as ballerinas.

Tiny illusionists, they rise and fall
on invisible sky-wires.

Millions of years after crawling from the sea,
they throw out nets to harvest the breeze.

They weave blankets for the ground's feet,
shawls for the quivering shoulders of the trees.

Their webs, transparent fielders' gloves,
pluck flies out of mid-air.

In this world they helped create, I am the newcomer
threatening, "Get out of town by dawn."

Yet—elfin bodyguards—they clear a path for me
through the constant crush of bugs;

they cordon off a spot—my private tuffet—
and they run away when I sit down.

## Once Bitten

It appeared after—he thought—a good night's sleep:
Faint tickling between pale arm hairs,
Redness moving in like headlights: twin
Spots, because what bit him had two fangs,

Though he didn't know this yet; he thought
He'd brushed some poison ivy, developed
An allergy. He never dreamed there'd been
A killer in his bed, even when the red

Turned gray, the skin collapsed like two sinkholes
Above the river of his blood. The doctor
Gave him cortisone, then ampicillin.
The tickling swelled to a bass throb.

Fire gnawed his wrist. Three specialists
Shook their heads until one old G.P.
Said "spider," and a Latin name. Everything
Blurred: the tests, the shots, the operating

Room, "strictly routine." When doctors pressed
A dive-mask to his face, he thought of Malibu,
Renting a surfboard, humming Beach Boy tunes,
Paddling out to where surfers bobbed

Like spiders on elastic bands. The waves
Seemed huge, but he thought he could ride
Until a big one tore the board out of his hands
And wrapped him, struggling like a fly in cold

Green silk. "My God," he thought, "I'm going to die
On my vacation." The idea made his mouth
Gape in amazement. Bitter as strychnine,
The whole ocean rushed in.

## One Story

It begins in Philadelphia, where the maternity nurse loves
the Philadelphia Athletics, who rarely win and will soon move
to Kansas City, taking their shortstop who gives C his nickname.
Or it begins on a Maryland dairy farm, where mornings smell
like flapjacks and manure, sausage and hay, where, of six
children, one dies of scarlet fever, one of whooping cough,
while three brothers and C's mother survive. Or it begins
in New Zealand: A boy, 14, ships out as a deckhand on a steamer
bound for London, where in three years, he'll meet his wife.

Agamemnon, a box turtle, is in the story—and one named
Inspector because he cranes his head to stare at C, and one named
Goof-Off because he bites, and one named Churchy after the
    turtle
in the comic strip C's mother reads to him. One day the thunder
sounds like God is pounding on the hull of a huge battleship.
One day the wind sounds like a python sliding through the trees.
A rock-and-roll band is involved, a smart kid—scorned by the
    Cool
Dudes—crowned overnight as the curtain rises on him, gripping
a red Gibson guitar, hamfisting through Freddie King's "San José."

Sometimes birdsongs outside C's room sound like creek-songs
winding through pasture, then scarlet maple trees. Look closely
and you'll see pillbugs bustling beside a wood-frame house,
a bristly wolf spider squeezing under the door, about to toggle
C's mother to scream, pressing the lever marked "Arachnaphobia"
in her son's brain. The story has the swirl and turmoil
of Van Gogh, the thrust and drive of Beethoven, the palette
of Matisse—cherry, coral, plum, indigo, saffron, amber,
lime, jade—though C will call them red, blue, yellow, green.

Highlights include a week fishing outside Kamloops, three-for-four
with a home run in winning the Oaks Dads Club pennant,
a divorce urged by a bitter therapist, a wedding interrupted

when a helicopter crashes in orange flames on the church lawn.
There are many love scenes—some better than others—
several loves, some of them "true." The story ends in a hospital:
C's son, daughter, and wife sobbing, an explosion of blood.
The story ends in a Nursing Home when C's 90-year-old heart
mercifully stops. The story ends in Moorea, tenth anniversary

of C's second wedding: rip-tide, panic, unconscious
drifting, sea-mouths wearing him away. The story ends—
its best parts still unconceived—with an engine roaring up a hill,
the author putting down his pen, rushing to trundle out his big
green garbage can to meet the fuming, beetle-browed black truck
twenty years before Agamemnon, who scaled C's chickenwire
turtle pen during a summer thunderstorm, and lived sixty years
in a vacant lot, is found by a red-headed boy, dropped
into White Oak Bayou, and floats all the way to Galveston.

## The Crane Boy

*Extreme isolation in early childhood causes children to have little or no speech and severely limited mental abilities. Although special training and regular attention can facilitate speech and intellectual growth after such children have been discovered, these children never reach their potential.*

*—from* Psychology, *by Lester A. Lefton*

He was not named for the bird—slow-flying,
legs like jointed straws—but for the long-necked
monsters, squeaky-tongued, that tear tenements down.
*Reek! Reek!* he cries, and slams his head against
the clinic door. He wants some moldy bread,

a cracked soap dish, sky-blue. (Who knows
if this is true? The party guest who said his name—
I forget hers—forgot what else she knew
about him, brother to the Teheran Ape-Child,
Lithuanian Bear-Child, Irish Sheep-Child,

Salzburg Sow-Girl—all those abandoned
by their kind, who, as another kind, survive.)
I see him chained to a commode
in a brownstone condemned and left standing.
Red jelly from his father's head spreads

on the street after a crack deal goes bust.
His mother clamps a charm between her thighs
to restore virginity. Rain rubs its cheek
against his window as he watches the cranes
batter buildings down. No one speaks to him;

but Wernicke's area, Broca's area
spark and sputter in the stinking dark.
*Reek! Reek!*—far back in his throat,

20

as if the sounds have fluttered over city blocks
or dropped from clouds like spiders on silk strands.

Maybe he means, "Don't hit me." Who knows
what he means: shit-glazed, back hunched, arms flapping,
head battering the wall. Maybe it isn't
what I think: pain of a man strapped down waiting
for cyanide; a woman paralyzed,

her thoughts strobe-flashing as her body calcifies.
Rescued, his eyes search for the cranes—squealing,
framed in soap-dish blue. When he says *Reek!*
maybe he means *Spider, kiss me.* Maybe
he means *I miss you, Mother Sky.*

## Girl at a Window

The moths which used to swirl like snow
Around the streetlamps, are gone.
Snow is gone too, since it's early spring.
And the rain which fell last weekend.
And the tulips which bloomed all day
Till night snuffed them like candles.

I stand hidden by curtains and watch you
Stride past the lamps into the black street
Gouged like a river through a battlefield.
It flows with corpses every workday.
Empty now, but still stinking of death,
It readies to carry you away.

You zip your coat as if keeping something in;
Fish in your pocket; find your keys;
Drop them. I hear the click,
See your head jerk as you curse
And stoop to pick them up. I watch
Unseen, the way I've watched you sleep.

You fumble with the lock, and slide into your car.
Still warm from me, smelling of me,
You're changing, as I am,
Elements reshuffling. What creatures
Will wear our clothes tomorrow?
What will they feel for one another?

I've read how, each dusk, Aztecs watched
The sun die—then, before each dawn, offered
Their gods human hearts, praying for a miracle.
We must pray for a miracle.
Here where everything dies, changes,
We must offer our hearts,

Bleed, sacrifice to feed love
And chase away the night. Though
In the end we need a miracle.
Each sunrise, heartbeat, breath,
Instant of love ends in a death,
Begins a miracle by flickering back again.

## Marilyn's Machine

She bought it because her baseball player didn't want her to,
because her playwright and her President and her Attorney
General disapproved. *You're a star,* they said: the one
thing they agreed on. *Stars don't wash their own clothes.*

Too timid to defy them, she rented a little room
and brought her purchase there, safe in its cardboard box.
Disguised in a black wig and flowered muumuu,
she sat and stared at the machine, imagining the famous

bras, nylons and panties, tight sweaters and skirts
sighing as they rocked, settling down into the warm
detergent bath. Sometimes she cried, thinking
of the men who dreamed about her clothes and what

went in them. How many orgasms had she inspired,
who'd never had one of her own, her breathy voice
warding off "Was it good for you?" She loved
selecting temperatures: hot/warm, warm/cold, cold/cold,

and her favorite, hot/cold. She loved the brand name
"Whirlpool Legend." She loved the cycles,
especially "Rinse" and "Spin." She whispered their names,
thinking of a man thinking of her some distant day

when she is nothing but an image made from movies,
photos, gossip, exposés—an image thinking of him
thinking of her in her black wig and flowered muumuu,
rinsing, spinning till the dirt is washed away.

# Fantasy Girl

"You're the fantasy girl, aren't you?"
—Bruce Willis to Jane March in *Color of Night*


Indian & Spanish? French & Chinese? Black & White?—
what collision of genes made this perfection that has just rear-
    ended you,
wearing a yellow scoop-necked blouse, eyes flashing diamonds,
voice a whisper, "I've got no insurance. Please don't bust my chops."

You can't help talking to yourself when she appears: "Here she
    comes,
wearing a backpack like a little girl, and falls into his arms."
It could be corny, but it's not because she's young and beautiful,
and nothing's corny about beauty and youth. Instinctively you
    know

it doesn't matter if someone leaves a diamondback in your mailbox,
if a red Ferrari tries to run you down, if you find a hose
flooding your living room, and stand on the veranda clutching
a butcher knife as tympani roar in your ears, and the house alarm

goes off like a scream. Later, as you clean up, harps will play
her theme and she'll appear. "Hi. Remember me?"—a breathy
intake after "hi" and "me," as if she's run a marathon. "There she is:
an angel dancing on the head of a pin," you'll say, transfixed

by her flowered dress through which a pubic halo gleams,
by lips and teeth so perfect they could be superimposed. Kissing,
she breathes, "Oh, oh," as porno music surges—strings and electric
fuzz guitar. You make love, slow-motion, in the swimming pool.

When the scene cuts to hang-gliders, it's not corny; and when she
    leaves you
strapped by one hand to the bed, you laugh; it's just enough
    depravity.

It doesn't matter if she fucks half of L.A., including women—
if she stabs her therapist thirty times, hangs an S & M freak by his
    heels,

carves "Rich Bitch" into his hide, and slits his throat—if she used
the same body moves, same whispers, same smile she's using on
    you.
It doesn't matter if she cooked for them too—*ahi* with steamed
greens and rigatoni perfectly arranged on white bone china—

if she wore the same ruffled French maid apron, nipples glowing
through, slim derrière (butt is too blunt; ass, too crude) with its
    rose
tatoo bared as she bends to pull perfect sourdough biscuits
from the stove—yours; she broke into your house to cook for you.

(Chimes in her theme now: sex and danger sautéed.) It doesn't
matter if she has multiple personalities: one a murderous boy,
one a slut who wears a gash of red lipstick, glittering hoop
    earrings,
mascara thick as tar. You know, because she's young and beautiful,

your worst suspicions can't be true. You know you'd enter hell
to save her, lightning flashing as you sneak past a gigantic
welded Jesus, then cages, clanking machines, griffins and krakens,
racks and screws. Satanic choirs can't mask the sobs

that glide down like wounded birds around you as you push—
through spiderwebs and blood—upstairs to find her, lash marks
on her back, hands nailed to her chair, driven psychotic
by her brother, crazed himself by child abuse: the only sin

the 1990s can't forgive. You know you'll face him
with his crucifying nails. You know that just as you saved her,
she will save you with a spike between his eyes as he's about
to sand off, inch by inch, your skin. You know his death will purge

her madness, but that someone so young and beautiful can't live
with fratricide, so she will climb—in thundering rain, as lighting

flickers like a faulty bulb—an iron ladder that beanstalks up.
You follow her, begging, "Come back." Souls in pigeon form
  explode

heavenward as, her wet shirt a sacrament, she stands on a roof
patterned like a waffle iron. She wants to jump—like someone else
you loved but couldn't save. This is your chance to be redeemed,
and so you plead, "Come back to me . . ." She reaches for you

like Eurydice. But death's wind flings her down, so you jump too,
catching a chain and then her arm as she swoops by, both
of you penduluming over the abyss where tiny car-lights cross
and twitch. You're not afraid; you know you'll swing her

to safety, then clutch each other in the rain as her theme rises—
strings this time—while lightning blinks off—on—off—on.
Your own madness broken too, you watch the credits to see
what name goes with so much beauty and youth. *Jane March?*

Absurdly plain. You hit rewind, pop out the tape, then plod
to bed and let your wife, with no gaffer to backlight a transparent
gown or bounce diamond-glitter off her eyes, with no director
to coax out each breathy line, with no shadowy, hellish past—

only the usual dark and tortured human history—to heat her kiss,
with only her arms, that would have pulled out of their sockets
if she'd dangled like Jane, to draw you back into her body,
back into this flawed and precious life.

# PART II

## Broken Toe

Blessings on you, toe of many colors:
purple as a grape, maroon as a raspberry,
yellow as a ripe casaba, greenish-white
as honeydew where the Doctor's adhesive pressed.

I've been boring lately, puffy little pig.
I've complained, "Nothing ever happens to me,"
swollen bread stick, stumpy penis gorged
with blood. I was sunk in complacency

with my good salary, good job, good girlfriend,
writing good poems about nothing (or next to)
not to offend the eight or ten good people
who read them. "Goddamn it fuck shit cocksucker

O Judas hump!"—it was a prayer you pulled from me,
fat gouty priest, when, in the dark, I tripped
on my Heater-Plus-Fan. "Motherfucking asshole
goddamn slutty shit-face, fuck fuck fuck!"

A word-orgasm after long celibacy. Bléssed release!
How did I stand the unfractured monotony?
Welcome back, pain. Welcome back, passion.
Welcome back, something-to-howl-about,

grist for the *how're-you-doing?* mill. Remind me
of the joys of walking, jump-rope, running,
playing footsie. Hammer home the certainty
of decay, memento mori at my body's end.

In the TV screen of your bruised nail, I see the usual
skulls and skeletons, but also wheelchairs,
triple-bypass surgeries, hit-and-runs,
cancers, deaths by earthquake, flood, and killer bee.

The words *fragility* and *tenuous* flow by
like banners towed by blimps. I wasn't drunk.
I kicked no woman, dog, or door, though if you like
to think I did, dear reader, do. Believe I broke

my toe drop-kicking ninjas, if it pleases you.
Simply to reach the fridge is an adventure.
I hop on one leg to answer the phone.
It took ten minutes, the first day, to get my shoe on.

When I found that I could not depress my clutch
and had to give up my day's plans,
I swore a good two minutes more, then hopped
inside, crimson with rage and pride—

with real conflict in my life—
with an ache so sharp that when I stepped
I cried, "Jesus!"—with my heart's silence broken—
with something to say.

# The Shape of History

*Turning and turning in the widening gyre . . .*

Today's paper is crammed full of news: pages and pages on the Somalia Famine,
the Balkan Wars, Gays in the Military. On this date a year ago, only 1/365
of "The Year's Top Stories" happened. *Time Magazine* fits a decade into one
thin retrospective. Barely enough occurred a century ago to fill one
sub-chapter in a high school text. 500 years ago, one or two things
happened every 50 years. 5000 years ago, a city was founded,
a grain cultivated, a civilization toppled every other century.
Still far ther back, the years march by in groups like grad-
uates at a big state university: 10,000 to 20,000 BC;
50,000 to 100,000 BC; 1 to 10 million BC. Before
that, things happened once an Era: Mammals
in the Cenozoic, Dinosaurs in the Mesozoic,
Forests in the Paleozoic, Protozoans in
the Pre-Cambrian. Below that, at the
very base of time's twisting gyre,
its cornucopia, its ram's horn
trumpet, its tornado tracking
across eternity, came what
Christians call Creation,
astrophy sicists call the
Big Bang. Then, for
trillions of years,
nothing at
all.

# In Praise of Pliny

He tells of headless people with eyes on their shoulders,
dog-headed people who bark, one-legged people
who hop fast, mouthless people fed by the scent
of roots and flowers, whom a stink can kill.

Twenty hours of every twenty-four, Pliny labored
to stuff into his *Historia Naturalis* "the contents
of the entire world." Servants read to him as he ate.
No time to waste, if he was to know how the elk-like

*achlis* has no knees, and so cannot lie down to sleep.
How it runs backwards dragging its huge lip.
How the *mantichora* has a lion's body, scorpion's tail,
and human face with three rows of fangs.

Of the moon, he writes, "now curved into the horns
of a sickle, now rounded into a circle;
spotted, and then suddenly shining clear,
vast and full-orbed, then suddenly not there."

Earth "belongs to men as the sky belongs to God . . .
lavishing what scents and savours, what juices, what surfaces
to touch, what colors." "Where," he wondered,
"did Nature find room in a flea for every sense?"

He tells how to choose good onions, and make glue;
how elephants write Greek, and hyenas call shepherds' names.
To cure a headache, he asserts, crush snails on the forehead,
coat the nose with vulture brains, wrap the temples

with rope used in a suicide. For toothache, gargle
boiled vinegar-and-frogs. For sneezing and hiccups,
kiss a mule's nose. For hair loss, dandruff, thin eyebrows,
rub with sulfur and bull piss. For any ailment: chicken soup.

When Vesuvius blew, Pliny—naval commander,
confidant of Emperors—sailed to Stabiae to save a friend.
He jotted notes as pumice rattled his friend's roof,
and snored all night. Next morning, pillows shielding heads,

his men struggled to launch their boat into high seas.
When flames and sulfur gas swept down, Pliny collapsed.
As he lay dying on the beach, could he have conceived
of people lacking all belief, devoid of wonder—

two-dimensional people who scoff at everything,
and swear their lives are wretched even as they roar
in horseless chariots across the earth he loved,
and soar in winged phalli through the enormous sky?

# True Prophets

Their speech doesn't sound prophetic:
"Wish the damn heat would let up."
"Do you carry three-inch finishing nails?"
Too late their wisdom becomes clear.

True prophets, though, care nothing
for their prophecy. It just leaks out
of them like garlic after Korean food.
Prophets adore food which is thoughtfully

prepared. Sometimes at a restaurant,
a prophet will leap from his chair,
shrieking with rage, or laugh for no
apparent reason, or weep uncontrollably.

This indicates a profound meal.
Prophets will speak of it for centuries,
and congregate where it was served,
although it rarely re-occurs.

Prophets love billiards, but play badly.
Whatever sparks their gift, extinguishes
their sense of angles and geometry.
They can shoot hours without sinking

a ball. When one goes in—even
the white—every prophet on earth
feels an orgasmic shudder. Sex
doesn't interest prophets much. Knowing

the outcome makes them lackadaisical.
This may explain their rarity. They mate
infrequently, and never with the same
person twice. What most upsets

a prophet is the so-called "hot-foot,"
in which matches are stuck between the sole
and upper of a shoe, then lit, causing
the victim to dance wildly and, if a prophet,

to fall into a trance from which he
or she can only be wakened by rapping
on the "funnybone." With the advent
of running shoes, however, and migration

of the populace toward video games, MTV,
and shopping malls, this method of "turning
a prophet," like prophecy—however true—
has ceased to have any significance at all.

## Twenty Years Late to See
## The Rocky Horror Picture Show

Brad and Janet, the square couple, are a hoot—
and the line "Didn't we pass a castle down the road?"
and Riff-Raff the hunchback, and his sister Magenta,
and of course the mad scientist Dr. Frank N. Furter:
a monument to camp, strutting and mincing in black corset
and fishnets, thick crimson lipstick, pearl necklace, purple
goggles of eye shadow, and a tattoo of a heart skewered by a knife
as he sings "I'm Just a Sweet Transvestite from Transexual
    Transylvania."

But what made the movie such a hit, and dates it so completely
as the 21st century closes in, is its atmosphere of pure
    permission—
"If it feels good, do it," from the days of Androgynous Rock:
Elton John in rhinestones and windshield-wiper specs,
David Bowie with his orange hair and Spiders from Mars,
Freddie Mercury and Queen, and my band, The Restaurateurs.
(We were thumbing through a dictionary, trying names
like Brünnhilde and Nepenthe, when someone read *restaurateur*,
and we all roared.)
                    The first time I wore lipstick
and green eye shadow, and stuffed a rolled-up washcloth
in my pants, I barely dared to step on stage. But people thought
we were rock stars, and pretty soon I thought so too, certain
we'd go platinum, reviling disco and *Saturday Night Fever*,
hot-tubbing with a blonde, brunette, and redhead all at once—
sweet, slutty innocents—years before Freddie got AIDS
and "We Are the Champions" became "The Show Must Go On."

That is why, watching *Rocky Horror* in my living room
on my VCR (a thing unknown when the movie appeared),
I listen, rapt, as Karen explains how the audience threw rice
in the wedding scene, covered their heads with newspapers
in the rain scene, flicked on their cigarette lighters

38

when Brad said, "There's a light over at the Frankenstein place."
That is why I grab my turtle, Excremento, in one hand,
and Karen's hand in the other, and dance with them
around my living room, and why all night the record-
changer in my brain plays and replays the sad hit single,
old as humankind: "Let's Do the Time Warp Again."

## My Muse

He's short—shorter than I—thinner, with frizzier,
redder hair: Woody Allenish, but gentile,
which makes it worse; he wanted Abdul Jabbar's
height, Schwarzenegger's muscles, Eastwood's face.
His skin is thinner than mine, too. He can't read
*The Times* without screaming. A distant mayoral race,

court ruling, car-jacking, mystery virus
makes him seethe. Picture the response to his own
termites, insurance hikes, full audit by the IRS!
He wrote a book called *Everyday Outrages*—
unpublished, naturally. He works as a lounge guitarist,
though he loathes club owners, Top 40, and drunks.

He's nearly scored eight record deals. (*The Tantalus
Predicament*, he calls it, hoping for a best-seller.)
He married a beautiful blonde, but she wanted him
to be "more mainstream"—i.e., rich. After two years
of monochromatic bickering, they divorced.
A year later, she's sharing a one-bedroom

in Topanga with an apprentice psychic surgeon.
"The main theme of modern life is the humiliation
of the protagonist," he likes to say. Actually likes to.
Left on my own, I could never invent a man
who, to stand out from the crowd, replaced his legs
with a calliope blaring "Darktown Strutters Ball."

I see a lightbulb as a glass shell surrounding
tungsten filaments, not a cell imprisoning a tiny
Thomas Edison, so irate his body glows. Lately
though, my muse has mellowed, or his level
of testosterone has dipped, or maybe he's worn out
from pummeling stupidities. At any rate, he's dictating

more words of praise, fewer of contempt.
He says that people need to hope more,
the less reason there is. He admits
he's been anorexic for acceptance,
bulimic for love. If he runs off and joins
a commune, my poems, will I still need you?

# The Reasonable Man

*". . . that staple of legal thought, the 'reasonable man' . . ."*
                                    —*Los Angeles Times*

He sets his radio alarm for 7:00, and jumps out
of bed at the first burst of Bach. This gives him
two hours to dress, eat Bran Flakes with skim milk
and half a pink grapefruit, then drive without speeding
to work. Except his olive Volvo won't turn over.

Damn—he paid three hundred dollars
for a five-thousand-mile service last Wednesday.
Good thing he kept the receipt. He calls
his law office to say that he'll be late.
The receiver looks and smells like hot French bread;

still, his call goes through. The answering machine
works perfectly—except Jill the secretary's
voice doesn't say, "Please leave a message";
it sobs, "I'm fat and miserable. Someone marry me!"
He leaves his message anyway, then dials Pete's Exxon.

Instead of Pete, he hears the thwap and chatter
of boys' baseball, a meadowlark's piccolo-trill.
His mom's voice calls, "Dinner's ready."
A baked-potato-sized lump lodges in his throat.
He gulps it down, picks up his briefcase—

shaped like a baseball bat—and locks
his house. Except the front door comes off
in his hand. His pants fall around his feet
and stick like bubblegum to his driveway.
And now the driveway is a river.

Billy Hill is splashing him. Carly Counselor
lolls on a humpbacked gray rock,
and calls his name. She's taking off her bra.
The river tops his nipples, rising.
Like it or not, he's going to have to swim.

## In the War Zone

I was asleep, face pillowed on the belly
of a famous swimsuit model, when the first
tortoise exploded in the street. Fragments
of carapace and plastron blasted through
the windows of my *pension* ("flop-house,"
my ex-wife called it). Red and purple innards
flecked the room. The tang of gunpowder
and reptile filled the air. The model—I can't
recall her name—galumphed around, screaming
for her dachshund. "Gretchen! Have you seen
Gretchen?!" "Is it on video?" I asked.
In the middle of the word *idiot*, the doorbell chimed.

It was the Buddhist monk next door.
His fat-lady patron had Gretchen wrapped
around her neck. "What's gotten into this mink?"
she snapped, punching Gretchen's yapping head.
"All submarines come from attachment,"
the monk said just as the next tortoise
went off, flinging us all to the floor,
making the monk's orange robe ride up.
He had the legs of a chorus girl, tied on
with string. I didn't know whether to laugh
or gag. The tug-of-war between the model
and the fat lady was stretching Gretchen

like a rubber bone. This reminded
me of lunch, which made me think how Mom
would stay up all night until I came home.
Her worried face looked "like a stuffed fish,"
I said to throw her off the scent of girlfriend.
Women's noses are more sensitive
than men's, giving them the kind of edge
I gained by smelling contraceptive jelly

as my wife slid into bed. I held her heart
as gently as a pet rat on those distant nights,
its velvet nose sniffing my hand,
not knowing I could crush it with a kiss.

## The Dead Run

Vampires and zombies, being liveliest, start first—
shambling, jogging, sprinting as their condition
permits. The freshly-dead in hospitals and funeral
homes totter to their feet (if they have feet)
and, embalmed or not, start running. Corpses claw
up from the ground, in the order they went in:
skeletons and rotted horrors hobbling and clattering,
stooping to pick up parts that fall. The long-dead
rise as human dust clouds, and run with the rest:
dark, stinking wind that crosses water as easily as land.

And now the oldest rise, the ones whose atoms
have mixed with everything. The Watson house,
the Pomeroy's sweetgum, Dottie Tang's azaleas
dissolve to let them out. Robert Ufman, Jan Nash,
Tiffany the Schneider Schnauzer disintegrate,
along with the still-solid dead, their molecules
joining the marathon that circles the earth
like a jet stream, until only I am left, remembering
how this always happens—how, in despair,
I pull a rib from my side, and begin again.

# Eating

*We eat. We are eaten. Wonderful!*
        —the Vedas

Always there must be the taste of pain:
Something ripped open, something torn apart
And ground between rough stones, something sliding
Down a dank passage into blackness, gnawed
By acid and enzymes with elfin names—
Ptyalin, Pepsin, Trypsin, Lipase, Amylase—
Then trundled down the bowels' coiled conveyer
Belt to squeeze out as a stinking sludge.

Always there must be the reek of death:
Something decapitated, felled by a hammer
Between the eyes, dart from an air-gun,
Bullet to the brain—something blasted
From the sky, pierced by an arrow, tracked
Bleeding through the snow—something jerked
Up by the roots, torn from its mother, hacked
Off at the thigh with leaves attached.

Something's life is poured into another's cup,
Leaving the drinker bloodstained, tainted
With the steam of rot. No wonder
I rejected what was gooshy, clotted,
Full of lumps. No wonder I spit up
In my high chair. I sensed, behind my grinding
Teeth and growling gut, worms chewing,
Germs' fanged mouths yawning to swallow me.

## Umbrellas

Miles of yellow parachutes-on-sticks,
pencil-necked mushrooms, buttercups
blown inside out—all popping up
on the curved arm of Highway 5.
The same thing, in blue, erupting in Japan
on the same day, like bilateral boils.

But prettier. It's art. The artist—Christo?
Cristo? Crisco?—pumped in six million
of his own dollars, cash. Twice
that many people came to gasp and stare.
Cars flowed up and down the 5
like colored bubbles in an I.V. tube.

"A triumph!" the *Times* declared.
Then wind sucked one umbrella up
and blowgunned it across the road.
Speared a spectator in the chest.
Made front-page news. Now
the artist's pulling his umbrellas down.

Poor guy's depressed. He can't go on.
As if people don't die more ignominiously
every day: A paper cut turns gangrenous.
A vat of molten lipstick dumps
on someone's head. No telling what
conch shell may hold a black widow

poised to whisper, "Poof, you're dead."
Stand with me, my beauty, in the wind.
Let us think of Art and blood tests
before marriage, and how love may come,
at any instant, flying through the air
to pierce our neck or skull or lungs or heart.

# Optimism

Buddy, can you spare me a dime bag of it?
Every radio and minister and mom-&-pop
combo in town wails, "It's getting better
all the time," and all I see are graveyards
unrolling for miles. My boss gives me a raise,
tongue flapping like a pink slip in the wind.
My wife buys me a blue angora sweater.
All my chest-hairs scream, anticipating it
stripped off me like a Band-Aid in divorce-
court. The judge leads cheers; spectators
whack me with *Ms* magazines. President K
calls the recession "Kaput," as soldiers stack
derelicts on wheelbarrows aimed toward
black buildings painted with orange flames.

"Contents may have settled during shipping,"
the box says. Settled for what? Why won't
Southern Comfort gush from my golf cap,
and azaleas shake out of my hands? What
I'd give to say, "The TV works; that's something!"
I grope my head for some knob that will change
my life. All therapy boils down to this:
"Look on the bright side." (Blindness. Heat stroke.)
"Think happy thoughts." (Peter Pan fills
his diaper in a nursing home.) Even this tossed
salad you serve, love—what do I see in its hollow
crystal ball? Lettuce (Let us pray; we need to);
Onions (waxy balls of tears); tomatoes (blood-
relatives of Deadly Nightshade); mushroom clouds.

## Mastery

While Fourth of July hordes crowd Crowley Lake
in motorboats and cabin cruisers, dredging
bottom with their Power Baits and grappling-
hooks and strings of flashers long as freight
trains, yelling, "Any luck?" "Hell, there's no
damn fish in this hole!"—cursing the sales guy
at Sports Chalet, swearing they'll never buy
another *Field and Stream* or Spin 'n' Glo,
an old man wades ashore, stiff legs hoisting
him up onto the sand. Mobs of the skunked,
like shoppers nothing fits, hurl their array
of gear down in their vans, and sneer, "Catch anything?"
He smiles and says, in a soft voice—full of bunk,
they know—"I got a few. I guess I did okay."

## Holiday Inn

It stalks the city's outskirts like some wonder
on *Wild Kingdom*. Green-and-gold signs lure
bright-colored cars out of their schools to blunder
into its wide jaws where, uninjured,
they disgorge their laughing guts. Inside
are heated pools, sauna, Jacuzzi, cocktail
lounge, plush rooms with king-sized beds, wide-
screen TV offering "Hot Male and Female
Action." Your personal phone connects you
to the world through computers which, because
they care, provide meals, massages, new
clothes, even typed notes from Santa Claus,
   and only mention payment if you're déclassé
   enough to scorn their offer please to stay . . .

# Buyer's Remorse

*I'd hate to take a job teaching, then spend*
*my life trying to get out of it.*
                    —Mary Oliver

No sooner do the ruck of us declare
"I do," than we don't anymore. Go out
for football, and we who never dared
to stand up on a pair of ice skates, pout
that we can't play pro hockey too. The ink's
still wet on our tickets to France, and we
wish we'd picked Japan or, come to think
of it, Kauai, New Zealand, or Tahiti.
Open any one door and we're deafened
by the roar—loud as the sea swallowing Atlantis—
as other doors slam shut, and their wind
knocks us down. The serpent didn't hiss
    to Adam and Eve, "Hide your nakedness!"
    He wore his best suit, and whispered, "Look at this."

## The Temptations of Pinocchio

We see Satan in Foulfellow the fox,
seducing Pinocchio from school, then shipping him
to Pleasure Island, where he smokes and loafs
and nearly makes a jackass of himself.

But behind Geppetto's smile, the beauty
of the Blue Fairy, the cuteness of Figaro the cat,
Cleo the fish, the singing conscience
Jiminy Cricket, Old Scratch is cackling too.

Skipping to school that first day of his wooden life,
Pinocchio is skidding toward a land
where boys are named Percy or Fauntleroy,
and always mind their moms, and never cuss

or fight or get their clothes dirty or talk
with their mouths full; and then one day—
reading their Bibles, dabbing specks of crumpet
off their little vests—their faces flatten,

bodies shrink, eyes bulge, noses turn black.
They drop down on all fours, long, silky hair
sprouting everywhere except the thin shafts
of their paintbrush tails. When pudgy, perfumed

demons flounce in and drag them off to sell
to fat ladies who hug and slobber, feed them
chockies, then spank them when they poo-poo
on the rug, they don't fight back; but for some reason

their dog brains can't comprehend—even as Pinocchio
homers through a stained-glass window,
slides a dead rat under a girl's chair—they dream
of wolf packs tracking deer through snowy woods,

pulling one down, tasting its hot, panicked blood.
This excites them so much that, on their puffy
pillow beds, their legs twitch; their jaws snap;
they try to howl, and wake up hearing yap, yap, yap!

## Nature Poem

Mountains are high and jagged; pines are green and tall.
Streams are clear, and slosh through valleys, and crash
Down waterfalls. Trout with bloody rainbow-sides
Hide under rocks in the clear streams. Jays scream.
Chokeberries glow. Clouds billow. Sometimes
They rumble in like buffalo, black bellies full of rain.

Sometimes you're fishing in a valley while rain slicks
The rocks, and your wife crashes, sloshing,
Into the trout stream. Sometimes you're miles from help,
From home, seeing the bone jut out of her thigh,
White and jagged as cracked pine. Sometimes blood
Paints a rainbow line on the stream's side

As water rumbles by, steam billowing into the clear,
Chilling air. Sometimes your wife is screaming
As you stand above her, hundreds of feet tall, hiding your face
So she won't see you choking, see the green bile flow.
She's had affairs for years. She thinks you know.
She swears she's sorry, swears she won't look at another

Man again if you'll for Christ's sake help her, please.
Sometimes you feel as if a mountain has fallen
On your head. As if your skull is full of jays screaming
In pain. You have had trouble believing in good things.
Sometimes you have believed your wife to be the only good
Thing in your life, the sole solidity in a world changeable

As the surface of a stream, treacherous as rain-slick rock,
Ready to crush you like stampeding buffalo. Sometimes
The clouds have made a roof of ice so black it glows.
Sometimes they hurl down snow like gravediggers
After a hard day, who just want to get her buried and go
Home. That's when the poem gets interesting.

## Evil Genius

I love it when one finally breaks, and blubbers,
begging for his life. Watching demented
Dr. K—who slaughtered millions—scream
when tap water is flung in his face
(he thought it was his killer germs), I laugh.
Take that, Mr. Pritchard, who ran World History
like a Gulag Death Camp. Take that, Ms. Simpson,
who read my essay to the class, then said,
"This is exactly what I can't abide."

                    Die, Dr. K!
No, wait, I want to be like you:
each sentence laced with lethal irony,
my longish hair and low, soft voice seductive
as any snake. I want to be a prodigy
playing chess with human pawns, laughing
because the fools will never understand.
I want to be so smart no prison can hold me,
no one contradict me with impunity.

Strap me into double straitjackets,
lock me in a cage, wearing a hockey mask—
I'll still suck out your eyes and get away.
Recaptured, composure restored, I'll let you
launch me, frozen, out into deep space.
In a few centuries, or weeks, or days,
millions will be dying of boredom, needing me
to spark some drama, make external their self-hate.
I don't even have to tell you, "I'll be back."

# PART III

# Invocation to Allen as the Muse Euterpe

Rise up, Allen, and appear to me.
Wherever you are, with whatever muscled acolyte, appear
    barefoot, in flowing robes, playing your flute, lilacs and orchids
    in your hair.
Or come as Erato if you prefer, or Polyhymnia, or Orpheus's mom,
    Calliope.
Prance in leading a circus, if it pleases you.
Or walk in professorial and dignified: asp the Establishment took
    to its heart.

Scream through a microphone, or whisper in my ear (no tongue,
    please).
Come from the fifties, your best years, smelling of reefer and
    whiskey, gism and sweaty underwear.
Come help me celebrate my failings, to admit how much it hurts
    to be barely five-seven—I who dreamed of being six-foot-three.
Come with Carl Solomon, Bill Burroughs, Herbert Huncke-
    rhymes-with-junkie, who robbed you blind to feed his habit,
    got you jailed as a burglar, but you took him back.

Come from Columbia, freshly-expelled.
Come with your mother Naomi, whom you committed to Pilgrim
    State Hospital, who thought her husband and your *buba* were
    conspiring with Franco, Hitler, Roosevelt to kill her, whose
    lobotomy you authorized, whose funeral, which you did not
    attend, lacked enough males present to have a Kaddish read, so
    that later you wrote "Kaddish" for her.
Help me admit that I abandoned my parents when they got too
    sick and old and floated out of their right minds—that I
    dumped them—Dad, then Mom—on my sister, and blamed my
    strenuous schedule, my happening life: teaching, doing therapy,
    re-marrying, and of course writing poetry.
Help me admit how totally I've failed at that: in my fifth decade,
    without a major book.

Come, sweet sunflower, trailing your addicts and addictions.
Come sick with love for Neal and Jack.
Come rattling the *Playboy* interview where you sang the joys of
　　buggery.
Give me machinegun bebop words, peyote psilocybin Nembutal
　　jazz words to immortalize the way I cheated on my wife, made
　　her hate her goodness and solidity by proving they weren't
　　enough for me.

Help me express my shame, my greed, my pettiness—the one
　　grand thing about me.
Don't stop there. Help me quit griping and celebrate L.A.: its
　　corpse-blue sky,
its Bel air and Beverly hills, its gurus and gangbangers, beaches and
　　waves into which, diving, you taste seven million bowels.
Help me to surface beaming, with a turd-crown in my hair.
You who could love cold-water flats, cockroaches and bedbugs
　　(human and otherwise), come with your minor poet father, your
　　Buddhism and "first word, best word" certainty.

Help me to sing of Hollywood pushers and peep shows and aging
　　stars ground underfoot, of Angelyne, "famous for nothing," who
　　looks down like God on rush hour with her abuse-me eyes
　　above her continental chest's white divide.
Appear to me, Allen, railing against Moloch in anti-Capitalist
　　frenzy, fresh from hallucinogenic quests to Mexico and
　　Amazon, trailing visions of Whitman, Blake, and Piggly Wiggly
　　West.
Help me to be more than just me.
Help me admit in raving holy poetry that I protested Vietnam not
　　because of my high morals, because I was scared to go—

That I'm scared most of the time—that I lift weights and kickbox
　　trying to be less scared—
That when I had a prostate biopsy, I whined like a baby, and when
　　the needle bit, called the doctor a dickface, the nurse a whore.

Help me confess the whole fiasco with Carol Drake, how tenuous
   my potency can be, how much ass I've kissed in my life, how
   many miles of shit I've wolfed, how eagerly.
You owe me, Allen—I bought your biography. No, actually I was
   too cheap. My cousin in publishing sent it to me free. (A cousin
   in publishing, and still no book!)

I have no magnanimity of spirit. I don't want to embrace all
   human-kind. I don't like bad breath and b.o. I don't like scabies
   and TB. I especially don't like embracing men. Oh, I can do it—
   the hard bear-hug, the forced heartiness—I'm an L.A. shrink!
   But men feel so clunky and thick, clutching each other like bad
   dancers afraid to start waltzing around the room.
All so we won't look homophobic.
Come to me, Allen; I'm not afraid of you.
I know I have no breadth of vision and no depth. I know I lack
   heart. Give me a transplant. Please.
The instant I saw you in your white pajamas, 1970, thumbnailing
   your harmonium, braying in your love-fest hippie-beaded
   tuneless voice, leaping around, an awkward, shameless spaz,
   chanting and dancing, ecstatic, orgiastic, delighted, joyous,
   gleeful, gladsome, gay—really, truly gay—telling a thousand
   college kids about your lips against a black policeman's chest,
   begging "Please Master," encanting "Please Master," praising
   God "Please Master," I knew if you could face the world that
   way, with your pubic beard, bald rabbi's head, hideous black
   glasses, and bare, pudgy, queer soul, then anything was possible,
   even for me.

# Peaches

was her name—this fat lady who lived three houses down
from my family. She wore big flowery muumuus, and a scarf
around her head like that black lady on the pancake mix.
She held her face hard and tight, like it was packed with so much
   lard,
if she relaxed, it would've dripped like candle wax. She had a boy

named Elwin—albino, deaf and dumb and blind, eyes sunk
back in his head like marbles, rolling up. He pranced
when he ran, like a puppet on strings. He'd smash into things
and fall, but not as often as you'd think. He worked his way
into strange places—our shed out back, or underneath the sink;

it was all blackness to him. He cost me a year's growth,
Mom said, the day I found him in my closet like some drooling
ghost. I knew I'd rather die than live like him.
"He'll get run over for sure," all the moms said. They'd cluster
in our front yard, whispered words like *white trash*,

*welfare baby*, *It ain't right*, leaping like sparks into my ears.
I was forbidden to play in Peaches' yard, or ask
her for a trick-or-treat, but one day I had Cub Scout candy
to sell. She looked as if she liked to eat . . .
I went to knock, then heard moaning from her window.

"O God," Peaches groaned, "O Jesus Lord . . ."
She was naked on her back in bed, fat titties hanging down
on either side, and Elwin's head in the thick moss that curled
and crackled between her hippo-thighs. I couldn't tell what
he was doing, but I watched until she saw me, yanked him up,

and held him like a shield across her chest. "What you doin' here?"
she screamed. "Nothin'," I said, wanting to run. Her stare
froze me. "You think you're somethin', don't you, boy?"
"No ma'm," I lied. "Look at you," she snarled, so fierce I checked
to see my pants were zipped. "You've got your mom and dad

and that red two-wheeler with them trainin' wheels. Alls I got
is Elwin. All he's got is me. You get him took away, God'll take
somethin' from you, wait and see." That unfroze me. I shagged
for home like I'd been blasted by hell-fire. But as cicadas tuned up
for the night, their buzzes gusting through the trees, and I tried

to think what I should tell my mom, something rose out of my
    head,
surrounding me with heat and light like angels in the Bible do.
Maybe I was scared that I'd get spanked for trespassing
in Peaches' yard, or that I'd say bad words explaining
what I'd seen, or maybe I didn't want to risk God taking my new

Huffy bike from me, but in that glow behind my eyes, I saw
how Peaches lay in bed, her moon-face smiling and glad,
how Elwin clung to her like a monkey-baby at the zoo,
and even after Peaches got cancer, and she and Elwin moved
away, I never told until now what I saw that day.

## Back Flip

"Ten bucks says you can't do it," shrilled Zack Boles,
who didn't have ten bucks, but had a Junior
Gymnastics gold medal from the "Y."

Dad leaned his rake against our sweetgum tree;
lowered his hands, and sighed. His belly—soft
and rounded as a pile of leaves—flexed

with his knees before they straightened, shooting him
up higher than I could have dreamed, his arms
level with the ground, knees lifting to meet

his hands, which pulled his knees over his head
as he spun like a cam on a drive-shaft,
a Foosball-man on its shish kebab of steel.

For an instant he hung: a poor, tricked codger
upended in his chair, thin gray hair plummeting
straight down. I pictured him stretched

on the ground, spine snapped, heart burst,
white-coated medics mouthing, ". . . nothing
we can do." But he kept turning, his tuck

opening, legs feeling for the ground.
His feet hit hard. He staggered, took a half-step
back, arms shooting out like antennae—

a Victory V—as the lawn, a Texas sponge,
sprayed creosote into Zack's face,
and streams of crystal glory over me.

## Without Being a Wimp

*The new man is sensitive and shares his feelings,*
*without being a wimp.*
—from an ad for a men's support group

Raised with a British "stiff upper lip," I don't
advertise my sensitivity. Mendelssohn's
Violin Concerto makes me cry—in private;
Elvis's song "Old Shep" does too, though I never
had a dog. And Van Gogh's paintings. And Michelangelo.
And thinking of my mom and dad. And Chief
Seattle's speeches. When I see a bag man
raving in the street, I wisecrack fast,
so that I won't start shaking. "You're cold, man,"
guys have said, meaning to praise.
                                    When I was eight,
I hung Ty Cobb's picture above my bed.
"The Georgia Peach," greatest batter who ever
lived, his cold eyes crowing, "I'm the best.
Outa my way." I studied his face daily,
trying not to care if Christy Saunders hated
my red hair, or Mike Ditz jeered because,
besides baseball, I loved butterflies and books.

Mom gave me classics: *Oliver Twist,*
*The Hunchback of Notre Dame.* Dad fed me tales
of conquerors: Alexander, Caesar,
Babe Ruth, Genghis Khan. Dad liked to talk
about *his* dad, a sergeant in the English army,
killed in combat when my Dad was four.
"I'm for the British," he joked during TV
shows about the Revolutionary War,
and told how my granddad "campaigned" in India
and Africa, and got a saber-scar
the length of his left leg back when Brittania

ruled the world. I pictured him on a Bengal
elephant, or hunting lions on Serengeti plains
that stretched in front of him like green
and endless music that could make any man cry.
I saw the natives bowing, heard them call him
"Bwana" and "Sahib." I didn't know
about Imperialism then, or the Third World,
or Human Rights. I just wanted to live
in wild and gorgeous places that were mine.

Sometimes I dream of Granddad striding over
those lush, conquered lands. His arms are thick,
his chest hairy and strong. The scar on his leg
stands out like rope as he walks, sure
of his purpose, sure he's right, so unlike me,
picking my way through other people's rights,
more others springing up each second
as the birth bomb explodes and rivers choke
and the sick earth pulses and glows. No,
I'm not "cold," even though I've parked
in handicapped zones, don't give spare change,
and love the joke about the sex doll who,
instead of moaning, "Ride me, you big stallion,"
whines, "What about my needs?" Who doesn't
want to own his lover? Who wouldn't
steal a country if he could?

                          I think this,
though I know Chief Seattle was right:
"The earth does not belong to man; man belongs
to the earth." I still admire conquerors,
though when I meet people with their traits,
I despise them. I hate war, but I like
winning. The clunky old "Star Spangled Banner"

gives me chills, even after Vietnam
and audit by the IRS. To be a man
is to be a contradiction, hard and soft,
hot and cold, never to think only
the "right" things, feel only the "right" ways—
to know Granddad sometimes pitied the natives
he hacked down, felt scared, hated his officers,
cursed the British steel that pinned him
like a butterfly, held him tight as any
conquered tribe.
                   To be a man is to feel
these contradictions welling when you write
a violin concerto, song, or letter
to a friend, when you paint the Sistine Chapel
or a field of crows, or scratch your name
in wet cement, or conquer Gaul, or drive
a tank across the sand, or kiss your son,
or cry your lover's name before you sleep,
fighting not to be a wimp, feeling life
stretch out before you like a wild and gorgeous land
that is yours alone, and mine alone, and ours.

## Four-Wheeling

Driving off-road, watch for rocks out of the corner
of your eye. If you focus on them, they're like magnets;
you'll think boulders have minds, and all hate you.

It's like climbing a cliff, then wanting to jump;
like seeing a woman you know will wreck your life,
and saying Hi. The Imp of the Perverse,

Poe called it. New-Agers call it psychic law:
You move toward what you think about.
The paper screeches BEIJING FLU POUNDS L.A.;

an hour later, my throat's raw. (Yet I often think
of winning the Publisher's Clearinghouse Sweepstakes.
I visualize their block-long caravan swarming to my door,

champagne popping to a brass band as cameras roll.
*Are you Charles H. Webb, Ph.D.?* Last time I checked.
*You've just won 10,679,533 dollars.* Are you kidding?

*No, I've got your check right here.* It never happens.
Maybe if I sent my entry in?) Therapists cite
the self-fulfilling prophecy: Fearing Claudia will cheat,

Ted treats her as if she has—snarls over dinner,
comes home drunk, avoids sex until she's so miserable
that when Frank at the office says, "How about coffee?"

she walks to divorce court, straight from his bed.
Homer was blind, but sensed the presence
of fanged sirens, whirlpools, Cyclopses, witches

who turn people into swine. You have to know
danger is there, but not dwell on it.
Gorgons can't do a thing unless you look.

Trust your mirrored shield. Trust your third eye.
Trust your instinct. Trust The Force. Stay loose.
Easy does it. One day at a time. Turn and accelerate.

Feather the wheel. Watch the dust fly up behind you.
Don't think *boulder.* Don't think *ripped oil pan,*
Don't think *Goddamn it, stranded!* Don't think *Wham!*

## Behaviorists

A few miles from the Vatican,
where priests ponder the Trinity
and Transubstantiation
in towns like *Terracina*,
*Sabaudia, Fondi*,
peasants whose ancestors
prayed to Jupiter, Diana,
Mars, now pray to saints:
Jerome, who sheltered prostitutes,
and died nursing the sick;
Elmo, whose blue fire assures
sailors of God's grace; Cecilia,
whose martyred corpse did not decay.

If a girl takes a lover, a boy
spits blood, a man cannot move
his bowels, a family needs
a new roof or younger cow,
they offer food, wine, fine
clothes to a saint's statue.
If the problem goes away,
the saint is praised. If it persists,
the supplicant may stand
the statue on its head,
or dunk it in the chamber pot.

Local priests scream "Sacrilege!
Idolatry!" Peasants humbly
confess their sins. But even
speed-chanting Hail Marys
and Our Fathers to the quiet

click of rosary beads,
they plan a pork-and-pasta
feast for kind St. Clare,
another week in women's
clothes, hung by his heels
for ungrateful St. Antony.

# Blind

It's okay if the word goes with *Venetian;*
Who cares what Italians don't see?—
Or with *Man's Bluff* (a temporary problem
Healed by shrieks and cheating)—or with *date:*
Three hours of squirming repaid by laughs for years.

But when an old woman, already deaf,
Wakes from a night of headaches, and the dark
Won't disappear—when doctors call like tedious
Birds, "If only . . ." up and down hospital halls—
When, long-distance, I hear her say, "Don't worry.

Honey, I'll be fine," is it a wonder
If my mind speeds down blind alleys?
If the adage "Love is blind" has never seemed
So true? If, in a flash of blinding light
I see Justice drop her scales, yank off

Her blindfold, stand revealed—a monster-god
With spidery arms and a mouth like a black hole—
While I leap, ant-sized, at her feet, blinded
By tears, raging blindly as, sense by sense,
My mother is sucked away?

## How Lizzie Died

I saw your amber slash by the trashcan
and had to have you. Stripping off my sweater
the way you shed skin, I dropped it on you,
snuck you inside past my mother,
and unwrapped you like a gift. "Just for a week,"
I told myself, awed by your darting slingshot-
tongue, thin, tyrannosaurus forelegs,
wand-like toes, legs in a catcher's squat.

Two weeks later, I found you in your shoebox,
crawled on by the crickets you wouldn't eat,
your body—stiff as a stuffed alligator—
curved like a fishhook, a jai alai *cesta*,
a comma, half a heart, an Alpine horn
that groaned across Houston, Texas, so loud
and long I can still hear it in L.A.:
*Shame on Charlie Webb. Sorrow and Shame.*

## According to the Rule

She judo-chops my Adam's apple.
I pop her a straight right to the chin.

She clamps my ear in her bloody teeth, and tears.
I thrust my fingers in her nose and rip.

She grips my balls and twists them off like knobs of bread.
I ram my fist up her, and gut her like a fish.

She grabs a cleaver; chops my legs off at the knee.
I seize a hacksaw; amputate hers mid-thigh.

She takes a sledgehammer and pounds my brain to jelly.
I take a jackhammer and smash hers into mush.

This goes on until only our eyes and hands remain
unscathed. That is the rule.

We must always be left some means to mutilate each other,
and some way to cry at what we see.

# Spirits

*At night when the streets of your cities are silent and you
think them empty, they will throng with the returning hosts
that once filled and still love this beautiful land.*
                                        —Chief Seattle

No street is silent here; still, they return:
faint whispers underneath the bray of horns,
the *runh runh runh* of gunning cars.

Instead of manzanita leaves and dry white yucca
petals, paper cups, torn taco wrappers,
pages of the *L.A. Star* and *Swinging
Times* skip and flutter as they walk
in winter mist past rusty fire escapes
and dusty floors and barred apartment doors.

Instead of deer hiding in chapparal,
whores in skirts narrow as hatbands peer
from shadows, watching for big bucks. At Lucky's,
where pimps suck down pints of Häagen-Dazs,
they crowd the aisles, thin voices mingling
with the buzz of freezers and fluorescent lights.

They slide through alleys where pale boys
with hair in warrior-crests fight for needles
to jab in their skinny arms. They glide down Sunset,
watching hustlers—jeans tight across their wares—
lock quivering johns in come-and-get-me stares.

Unharmed by speeding Broncos, roaring trucks,
they drift through smog, searching for roadrunners,
kingsnakes, possums, live oak trees, wondering
where is the sea breeze that used to come
with morning fog? Where are the owls, the red-
tailed hawks that soared above their hunts, the bobcats,

75

tortoises, jackrabbits, skunks who gave them
power, were their kin in a boundless world
where everywhere was home.

                    Only at dawn,
when for an hour traffic ebbs, and crows
come back to crouch on streetlamps, and mocking-
birds sing up the sun just as they've done
for fifty thousand years, the hosts are soothed;
and here in Hollywood, where white men's
dreams are born, they shut their eyes
like babies calmed by mother's breast,
and settle down to rest, and sink,
like water into sand, beneath the concrete
that smothers this beautiful, lost land.

# Heat Death

"... the universe might eventually reach a temperature
equilibrium in which ... useful energy sources no longer
exist to support life or even motion."
                    —*New Grolier Multimedia Encyclopedia*

The stars will give up fusing hydrogen, spewing
helium into space. The clouds of dust six trillion
miles long in which people see plesiosaurs

or Jesus' face will stop condensing into stars.
The temperature in Mauna Kea and at Nome
will be the same. The temperature of a boy's

lips and a girl's breast will be the same.
The temperature of a song sparrow will be the same
as the temperature of the fog that made it puff

its feathers, trilling in my lemon tree.
Its small brown beak—bug-catching pliers—
will open no more. Heat death will come, of course,

long after the last glacier has vaporized,
the last boy and girl and song sparrow melted
into molecules. But I can't comprehend

a static soup of matter stretching endlessly.
To think of heat death, I must use human terms:
the edges of my curtains not glowing at dawn;

Miss Carol, my cat, not moaning to call hissing
Toms to my back yard; my arms, which ache
to pull you close, frozen forever at my sides.

## What the Poets Would Have Done for You

Homer would have burned a gold-fleeced lamb,
    bribing Zeus to clear his cataracts,
    then stolen you, although it caused a war.
Sappho would have fed you *mousaka* with *ouzo*,
    hoping you'd pass out in her bed.
Ovid would have wooed you with sexy hexameters.
    He would have said you were the earth,
    and he, a man partly transformed into a tree.
Chaucer would have called you "sweet Criseyde,"
    and gotten lost on a pilgrimage with you.
Shakespeare would have jilted his Dark Lady,
    and revised *Hamlet* as *Ophelia the Dane.*
Donne would have tried to seduce you in 1610,
    to convert you in 1615.
Swift would have hidden to watch you undress for bed,
    then swiped your chamber pot.
Keats would have lived past twenty-six.

Poe would have hooked you on opium,
    and re-named you with long "U"s and many sighs.
Swinburne and Tennyson would have vied to create
    the most honeyed euphemism for your tongue.
Yeats would have wooed you
    with a silver apple of the moon,
    won you with a golden apple of the sun.
Eliot would have done exactly as J. Alfred Prufrock
    would have done.
Pound would have gone bonkers for you.
Berryman would have killed himself—maybe for you,
    maybe not.
Sexton and Plath would have killed themselves in spite
    of you.

I would have written better, if I'd had the gift:
  made aspens quake with my love sighs;
  plucked diamonds from the clear metal of trout streams,
  and changed them from a metaphor into a ring.

## Reading the Water

You have to know cascades and rapids,
  Runs and riffles, flats and pools,
    The places where trout ambush food—

    Behind a rock or sunken log
  That breaks the current, underneath
An overhanging bank or shrub,

In gravel trenches, at the still
  Seam where currents sew together.
    You have to know what color means:

    The gold of shallows, the deep green
  Of water holding fish. You have
To know the languages of streams:

Mountain creeks gurgling through ferns,
  Spring creeks oozing earth's clear blood,
    Meadow streams snaking through lowlands

    While cows wade and crows jeer,
  Freestone rivers—cobbled highways
To the sea. You have to know

How to probe the pocket water
  And weed flats, to work a riffle's
    Head and tail as it twists in its stoney bed.

    You have to know the sheltering lies
  Where trout hide from their enemies,
The holding lies where they can rest,

The prime lies where lunkers brood
  Like sulky kings, the empty water
    You can flail all day, foolish

As Darius lashing the sea.
You have to know where mayflies hatch,
Where caddis nymphs trundle their pebbly

Caves ashore, where stoneflies crouch
And gnash their jaws, where midges swarm
Like winged commas tossed from a printer's tray.

You have to know the glades where nyads
Comb their hair and play, the pools
Where water eases pain and dissolves years.

You have to know what the rain dreams
As it lies sleeping in the clouds,
What mountains say as lightning flashes

Peak-to-peak. You have to know
Where sunlight hides when night's cold
Current covers you, your heart a boulder

In a black stream, and how to read
The poem the moon inscribes in silver
On the dark rush of your soul.

## Poem for the Future

Five years after Anne and I divorced,
fifteen after her father's aorta
burst like a water main in the mountain
cabin where he went weekends to drink,
I still use his pencils, printed:
              *Left on Purpose by:*
                   JACK WIGGINS
               FISHER FLOUR MILLS
                 Quality Feeds

I read his message as I jot my grocery list
and scribble a note to my new girlfriend—
"Taking shower. Come on in."
Grading Compare/Contrast essays
in the nearly occluded heart of L.A.,
I hear, instead of braying horns
and growling jets, the bleat of sheep
and cluck of chickens; I breathe
the dusty warmth of oats and wheat
and cornmeal puffing out of burlap bags;
I see farmers in John Deere hats,
beefy wives shepherding towheaded flocks.

Jack's pencil serves in many ways:
professor's pointer, Ninja hand-spike,
conductor's baton, and today
imagination's censer, filling
the smoggiest air with the sweetness
of straw and animals and dung:
a scent so close to human hearts,
we link it to a god who left his son
in a manger on purpose to comfort us,

just as Fred, my turtle, left his shell;
Anne, her memory; and Jack,
his pencil with which I write this,
*Left on Purpose by:*
CHARLES H. WEBB

## A NOTE ON THE AUTHOR

Charles Harper Webb grew up in Houston and was educated at Rice University (B.A.), the University of Washington (M.A.), and the University of Southern California (M.F.A. and Ph.D.). He worked for fifteen years as a professional rock singer/guitarist, and is currently a licensed psychotherapist as well as Professor of English at California State University, Long Beach. His poems have appeared in *American Poetry Review, Iowa Review, Michigan Quarterly Review, Paris Review, The Best American Poetry, 1995,* and many other magazines and anthologies. He edited *Stand Up Poetry: the Anthology* (The University Press, CSULB), and has published a novel, *The Wilderness Effect,* with Chatto & Windus in the U.K.

## A NOTE ON THE PRIZE

The Samuel French Morse Poetry Prize was established in 1983 by the Northeastern University Department of English in order to honor Professor Morse's distinguished career as teacher, scholar, and poet. The members of the prize committee are Francis C. Blessington, Joseph deRoche, Victor Howes, Ruth Lepson, Stuart Peterfreund, P. Carey Reid, and Guy Rotella.